A Month of Meditations for
WOMEN

A Month of Meditations for WOMEN

DIMENSIONS
FOR LIVING
NASHVILLE

A MONTH OF MEDITATIONS FOR WOMEN

Copyright © 2003 by Dimensions for Living

This book is printed on acid-free elemental-chlorine–free paper.

ISBN 0-687-02641-5

Meditations in this book were compiled from *365 More Meditations for Women,* copyright © 1992 by Dimensions for Living. Reprinted by permission.

Meditations 5-6, 8-10, and 12-14 were written by Lenoir H. Culbertson. Meditations 4, 7, and 11 are adapted and excerpted from The Sanctuary for Lent 1991 by LeNoir and Barry Culbertson. Copyright © 1991 by Abingdon Press. Reprinted by permission. Meditations 18-19 were written by Becky Durost Fish. Meditations 24-25 were written by Mary Ruth Howes. Meditations 2-3 were written by Maxine Dowd Jensen. Meditations 26-31 were written by Anne W. Killinger. Meditation 1 was written by Marjorie L. Kimbrough. Meditations 20-23 were written by Rebecca Laird. Meditations 15-17 were written by Shirley Pope Waite.

06 07 08 09 10 11 12—10 9 8 7 6 5 4 3

MANUFACTURED IN THE UNITED STATES OF AMERICA

1

Meditate on John 21:15.

A little girl once asked her grandmother if she loved her as much as she did the other grandchildren. The grandmother explained that she had a corner of her heart especially for each of her grandchildren and that she loved them all the same. As additional grandchildren and great-grandchildren were born, the grandmother's heart just kept getting bigger so that more corners could be added. Loving hearts are like that—there's always room for one more.

Every time I think about that little girl's question, I wonder whether the child really wanted to know if her grandmother loved her as much as the others or more than the others. You see, we all want to be the favorite, the one who is the recipient of the most love.

Even Jesus asked Peter, "Do you love me more than these?" (John 21:15). Although Peter answered affirmatively, Jesus asked him a second and a third time if he loved him. You see, Jesus needed to determine the extent of Peter's commitment to service. Those who love the most are required to work the hardest. Those who move more than these must let their light shine the brightest. Those who love more than these will feed his sheep.

When the little girl asked her grandmother if she loved her as much as she did the others, that little girl wanted her grandmother to feed her, to show her the affection that only a grandmother could give. That little girl wanted her grandmother to make a commitment to service. She wanted to see the light of love in her grandmother's face. She needed to be assured that her special corner would not be given away. If all else failed, that little girl wanted to know that her grandmother's open arms would welcome her in love.

If we love more than these, we give more. We let our light shine more. Do you love him more than these?

———

2

Meditate on Micah 4:4-5.

When I was a teen I wondered about many things I read in the Bible. One of these was when Christ told Nathanael he'd seen him "under the fig tree" (John 1:48). From time to time, I'd try to picture what Nathanael did under that tree. It couldn't have been something bad since Christ didn't seem to be rebuking him. Nor did Christ refuse him admittance into the special group of twelve. Micah 4:4 says that many shall sit there, and when they do, "no one shall make them afraid."

Recently my minister mentioned Nathanael and his fig tree in a message, so I asked him about it.

He said that "under the fig tree" meant to study the Scriptures, to be seeking answers, to be interested in holy things. In theological seminaries it has become a catch phrase: "I can tell you've been 'under the fig tree.'"

How many times does God see us there? Is it only when we have cause to be afraid?

I'm determined to spend more time there—not just when I'm worried or in some other kind of need.

How about you? Do you want to know more about God and obtain answers to the mysteries in the Scriptures?

Lord, help me spend more time with you, learning and understanding the messages your word has for me so that others may know I've been alone with you.

3

Meditate on Haggai 2:1-5.

Some of us have unfinished business in our lives, just as the restored remnant saw only part of the temple. Haggai's task was to encourage the people to complete the project.

As a child, I started many handcraft pieces and stopped before they were finished. When a hard task confronted me, I sometimes gave up. My mother had an adage she hoped would spur me on: "God helps those who help themselves." Haggai had a similar one for his people: "be strong . . . and work: for I am with you" (KJV). When I read it, I thought of my mother.

It took me twenty years to finish my first afghan. I started it before I ever began my first job, so I didn't have enough money to buy all my yarn. After getting a job and seeing my fellow employees knitting at noon, I dragged it out again. When I was transferred to another office, I put it away. But after marrying, I knew my husband needed something to cover him when he napped on the sofa. So I finished it, twenty years later.

Other things are unfinished in our lives. There may be a sister from whom we are estranged. Our parents may have fought against our marriage and we have turned our backs on them. A former friend may not even know the reason we stopped seeing her.

Unfinished people business can poison our lives, make us less than we should be, stop us from doing certain tasks.

Why don't we decide to be strong and work toward a reconciliation? God will be with us as he was with Haggai and the restored remnant.

———

Meditate on Ephesians 3:20-21*a*.

How marvelous is the gift of imagination! My friend Suzanne told me about a picture her little girl drew for her at age two. It basically consisted of one large purple blob in the middle of the page.

"That's nice, Katie. Can you tell me about it?"

"It's a house and two cows."

"I think I see the house here, but where are the cows?"

"Mom, they're behind the house!"

That's imagination! Victor Hugo once said, "There is nothing like a dream to create the future." That's imagination, too, for to imagine is the first step toward making something real.

Thomas Edison had to imagine the lightbulb before he could begin the long process of designing one. Alexander Graham Bell had to imagine the telephone before he could ever come close to assembling one. Abraham Lincoln had to imagine a

13

unified nation with freedom for all before he could work toward establishing one.

Imagination is the first step toward making something real, and in this sense the church is a community of imagination. Jesus came into the world, and through his life and death and resurrection, he has called us to imagine the kingdom of God—a kingdom of righteousness, justice, and peace. When we can imagine it as real, we are taking the first step toward living it as real.

But imagination takes effort and demands that we see beyond what is to what may be: God calls us to use our best gifts of imagination to awaken the reality of the kingdom of heaven in our midst.

———

5

Meditate on Matthew 6:34.

On a beautiful warm sunny day, a friend of mine was mowing the lawn when suddenly a large maple tree crashed to the ground, crushing the lawn mower just inches in front of him. After taking several moments to recover from the shock, my friend began to inspect the tree, searching for some clue as to why this seemingly healthy tree, for no apparent reason, had splintered right before his eyes.

Before long, he discovered the reason. Years before, someone had used what was then a straight little sapling as an anchor for a clothesline. Over time, the tree grew and hid the metal wire from sight, but nonetheless, it continued to cut at the heart of the wood, leaving it weakened. The day came when the weakened center just could not bear the weight of the tree any longer.

Human life is a lot like that. Anger never resolved, some hurt never consoled, some loss never filled, some sin never forgiven—these things cut deep within us, and even when we can put on a smile and say, "Oh, I'm just fine," the constriction continues to weaken the very core of our being. Sometimes our lives come crashing down, not because the weight of today is too great for us, but because the hurt of some yesterday never let us grow properly in heart and mind and spirit so that we could adequately deal with today.

"So do not worry about tomorrow, for tomorrow will bring worries of its own. Today's trouble is enough for today" (Matthew 6:34). Perhaps these words of Jesus are a reminder not to worry so much about tomorrow, but they also are a reminder to be sure that we address all that comes to us today.

6

Meditate on 2 Timothy 1:7.

After years of dreaming, a friend of the family finally made it to the Big Apple to see the New York Yankees play ball. An inning or two passed, and he became curious about a uniformed man who walked up and down his section of seats, shouting, "Skunk eyes! Get your skunk eyes!" Finally he waved the man over, curiosity getting the better of him, and said, "Let me try some of those skunk eyes."

"Skunk eyes?" he shot back. "I'm selling score cards." (Northern and southern accents must be added by the reader!)

I think of those "skunk eyes" from time to time when I feel that God is leading me, often pushing me, to take up some new task or put aside some old routine. "God," I think, "surely I'm not hearing you right. Surely you don't want me to do that?"

How do we know we are understanding the will of God for our lives? What are the steps toward discernment?

In 1947 Albert Edward Day wrote *Discipline and Discovery*, a little book that helped me to more fully understand that spiritual disciplines allow a person's life to remain open to God and thus discover the will and purpose of God.

What are spiritual disciplines? They are simply things we can do that enable us to push aside the clutter of life and make a space for God in our hearts. The traditional disciplines are obedience, simplicity, humility, frugality, generosity, truthfulness, purity, and agape love; but one could also add things such as study, prayer, confession, and worship. The form is not nearly as important as the results—hearing God more clearly and being gracefully empowered to act upon that which you hear. As James Fenhagen noted in his book *More Than Wanderers*, "A life of inner discipline is not only the result of faith, it can lead to faith just as we learn the meaning of love by loving. Our task is not to search for God, but rather to open ourselves to the reality of God's search for us."

7

Meditate on Matthew 7:7.

I don't know at what point students learn this, but it must be in a standard 101 level course that we learn to smile, nod our heads, and write knowingly in our notebooks when we *haven't got a clue!*

"I didn't know you didn't understand; why didn't you ask me?" the teacher will say. We have no good response.

Why are we afraid to ask questions? And, more important, why are we afraid to ask questions of God? Is it an admission that we are not perfect? (God already knows that!) Is it that we fear God will reject us? (God in Christ has promised to be with us "even unto the end of the world"— Matthew 28:20 KJV.) Is it that we think it's not respectful? (Do our children ask a thousand "whys" because they don't respect us or because they come pre-packaged with a thousand questions?) Is it that we don't think God can handle it? (God is not us, God is *God*—creator and sustainer of all things. Perhaps God is even the author of our questions.)

Any teacher can tell you that a key to true understanding is a good question. And how God hungers for us to truly understand, to be released from fears, to move, in God's time, from seeing "in a mirror, dimly" to seeing face-to-face (1 Corinthians 13:12).

———

Meditate on Romans 8:35, 37-39.

Children have a refreshing, if not shocking, way of looking at the world. This is so, in part, because they are looking at things fresh and are not yet bound by a host of carefully prepared presuppositions.

I was shocked into taking a fresh look at my faith recently while riding in the car with my four-year-old son. "Mom," he mused, "if there were no earth and no space, we'd all have to stand on God's head. Right, Mom?"

At first I was a little concerned about the state of his religious education, but as I thought about it, I came to wonder if in his young heart he was not trying to express the same kind of affirmation of faith that the writer of Deuteronomy made when he declared, "The eternal God is your dwelling place, and underneath are the everlasting arms" (Deuteronomy 33:27 RSV).

How wonderful to know, beyond a shadow of a doubt, that no matter what twists and turns life

21

takes, regardless of both the predictable and the unpredictable circumstances of life, no matter what, underneath are those everlasting arms of God, bearing us up, leading us forth, and guiding us toward life.

This is the assurance Paul tried to relate to the church at Rome in their time of trial:

> Who will separate us from the love of Christ? Will hardship, or distress, or persecution, or famine, or nakedness, or peril, or sword? No, in all these things we are more than conquerors through him who loved us. For I am convinced that neither death, nor life, nor angels, nor rulers, nor things present, nor things to come, nor powers, nor height, nor depth, nor anything else in all creation, will be able to separate us from the love of God in Christ Jesus our Lord. (Romans 8:35, 37-39)

I hope that in the years to come, I'll have the opportunity to say to my son, "See. You were right. No matter what, God always gives us a place to stand."

9

Meditate on 1 Samuel 16:7.

Following extensive knee surgery, I entered what was to be months of physical therapy. I remember so vividly the day I finally "graduated" to the stationary bike, with the instructions to just rock back and forth on the peddles. Peddling a full 360° turn was weeks away! While I was sitting there, carefully rocking back and forth, another patient walked past and casually declared, "You're not going to get too far!"

I smiled, but inwardly that casual comment hurt. He didn't know just how far I had come or how hard I had worked just to get to the point of sitting on a stationary bike, rocking back and forth.

How quick we are to judge others without knowing the battles they have faced or the struggles they have endured before their life came into our view. How quick are we to judge ourselves by vague standards of "getting there" that may or may not fit our journey. Is the value of a life something that can be judged in terms of destinations alone?

Christ Jesus came into human life to say, among other things, that there is another dimension of value that comes from beginnings: whose we are. We are God's sons and daughters, and wherever we go, wherever we find ourselves, we have a Companion and a Friend.

———

10

Meditate on Psalm 51:7, 10.

When I was doing the dishes the other day, I picked up a blue and white plate that my husband and I had received as a wedding present. As I plunged it into the soapy water, I began to wonder just how many times I had washed that same plate. Over the last fifteen years, I'd seen it serve Sunday pot roast, and I'd seen it serve peanut butter and jelly sandwiches. I'd seen it sparkling and new as it came out of the beautifully wrapped package, and I had seen it after it had been under the couch for a week, gleaming with all sorts of colorful mold. I had seen it at its best; I had seen it at its worst. But even at its worst, I'd always been able to submerge it in the suds and make it clean again.

I guess God must wonder about me in a similar way. "How many times have I needed to wash that soul clean?" God has seen me at my best and at my worst. God knows how often I have fallen short, and yet God continues to see another reality of what I may yet become in grace. So when I offer myself to his forgiveness in love, he makes me clean again.

This can be a new day, a new beginning, a morning as fresh as spring, if we pray, *Lord, once again, make me clean.*

11

Meditate on Psalm 46:1-3.

It has been said that nothing is as permanent as change, and change certainly is common to us all. We expect some changes with the flow of life, as we move from adolescence to adulthood, from singleness to marriage, from life as parent to life as grandparent. Some changes come "on schedule," but then there are those unforeseen changes that rip and pull at our lives until we hardly recognize them as our own. God's promise is that in the midst of all the changes we expect, as well as the changes that shake us with the fury of an earthquake, God is ever there—our refuge and our strength—a stronghold upon which to stand firm when everything about us appears to crumble and fall.

But that word *refuge* also denotes a habitation—a home, a place not unknown or foreign to us. It is not a distant castle, not a hotel, but a home with which we are familiar, a home to which we have the key to open wide the door—a home where a welcome is always prepared for us. God is a stronghold. God is home.

———

12

Meditate on Matthew 5:6.

I was serving Communion one Sunday morning when I approached a boy about ten years old. Watching me lean toward him, the boy threw up his hand and said, "I don't want any today. I'm not very hungry."

What a parable for the way many of us approach the table of Christ, the place where we are called to remember the life, ministry, death, resurrection, and continuing presence of Christ. How many times do we push aside the blessings of God with the words, "I'm not very hungry"?

Why are we not hungry for the true food of righteousness, justice, and purity? Perhaps it is due to the fact that we fill ourselves with spiritual junk food, such as: "But I'm not as bad as they are," or, "Everybody else is doing it," or, "If it feels good, I'll do it."

No wonder Jesus preached, "Blessed are those who hunger and thirst for righteousness, for they will be filled" (Matthew 5:6). It is hard for the blessings of God to fill us if we don't even know that we are starving.

———

13

Meditate on John 15:5.

One spring we discovered a great big pear tree full of blossoms behind our house, but as summer came, the only thing the tree produced were a few hard, inedible pears. "Maybe next year it'll be better," I thought. But the next year brought the same results. We found out that the tree was dying at the roots. It couldn't produce much because it was disconnected from the source of its life.

I couldn't help recalling the words of Jesus: "I am the vine, you are the branches. Those who abide in me and I in them bear much fruit, because apart from me you can do nothing" (John 15:5).

I began to wonder about my "root." Did the "fruit" I was producing in my life indicate that I had a healthy connection with my roots?

Branches bear fruit consistent to the species. Is my fruit consistent with my roots in Christ? How about your life? When other people encounter your life, do they encounter "fruit" like that which was produced when lives encountered Jesus? When people know you, really *know* you, do they also come to know that kindness is stronger than cruelty? That mercy is stronger than revenge? That right is stronger than wrong? That hope is stronger than fear? That love is stronger than hate? That God is stronger than the past and that in Christ we and the whole world are being made new? Common roots—good fruit!

———

14

Meditate on Matthew 5:13-16.

In the life, death, and resurrection of Jesus, God had a plan. And the plan was *us*—you and me! The plan was that just as Jesus was the light of the world, so also are we to be light. Just as Jesus was satisfying and purifying salt, so also are we to be salt. What a great trust placed within our hands!

But must we not confess that often we have taken our saltiness and applied it in places that were already salty enough? Often do we not add our light were lights are already glowing? It is easier that way. It's safer that way. But doesn't the voice of God whisper, "Go, in the name of Christ, to the tasteless wilderness—they need your salt. Go, in the name of Christ, and brighten the dark corners of despair and hurt—there are so many out there and your light is needed there."

Where are those places in the world that need your salt and light? You can name them. Go! Infuse your life and let your light shine. The presence and the promise of God will go with you.

———

15

Meditate on Jeremiah 29:11.

The story is told of a young woman who won a trip to a large city. She had never been out of her native mountains, so she looked forward to staying in a posh hotel and taking in urban sights.

Upon her arrival at the hotel, a man said, "I'll show you to your room." She followed him inside a door and was devastated. Why, this was nothing like what she had imagined! No furniture, not even a window. She expressed her disappointment to the man. He shook his head and said, "Ma'am, this is the elevator!"

The story reminds me of a friend's recent experience while attending an international convention. A hotel elevator full of women from the 32nd floor kept stalling between floors. Each time the door opened, the women saw a blank wall. When the elevator finally opened to daylight, all of its occupants got out on the 20th floor and walked the rest of the way to the lobby.

God speaks to me in two ways through these illustrations. I often jump to conclusions before God has a chance to show me what he plans for my life. Second, when I hit a blank wall, I may have to change direction, even if it's more work than I first anticipated.

In the elevator of life, I have a choice—I can push the UP button and go up in my spirit with the Lord, or the DOWN button and find myself down in the dumps.

Father, how glad I am that you do have plans for me. If changes need to be made in my life, help me to be flexible.

———

16

Meditate on John 8:12.

I always chuckle when I think of the story of a man driving in fog. Unable to see the road clearly, he followed the taillights in front of him.

The lead vehicle turned and then stopped suddenly. The second driver ran right into the back of the first car. He jumped from his car, yelling, "What do you think you're doing, slamming on your brakes?" Whereupon the first man replied, "What are *you* doing? I just turned into my driveway!"

That little anecdote tells me something. When I'm in a "fog" and not sure of my direction, I must be careful whom I follow!

Today there are many groups clamoring for my attention. Some look so authentic that I might be inclined to heed them. But I must keep my eyes on the One who calls himself the light of the world, for when I do, he promises I'll never walk in darkness.

Father, when I don't know which way to turn, please open my eyes to your light so that I will always follow you.

―――――

17

Meditate on Galatians 5:22-23.

Apples are a big crop in Washington state. In fact, we rank first in apple production for the nation. Recently an annual crop produced almost five billion pounds of apples, worth $282 million, with our Walla Walla Valley contributing $30 million of that amount. The Yakima and Wenatchee Valleys vie each year for the title of "Apple Capital of the World." Red and Golden Delicious, Rome Beauty, Jonathan, Granny Smith, Gala—the list could go on—Washington's valleys produce the best fruit.

I've found that to be true of my own valleys. The best growing conditions for spiritual fruit are often found there. As I rely upon the soil and sunshine of God's love in my "valley" times, he changes my

hatred into *love*
sorrow into *joy*

worry into *peace*
intolerance into *patience*
rudeness into *kindness*
envy into *goodness*
unbelief into *faithfulness*
grouchiness into *gentleness*
temper into *self-control.*

Whatever circumstances await you in your valleys, let God transform them into the fruit of his Spirit.

Thank you, Master Gardener. Cultivate my soul that I may show forth your precious fruit.

———

18

Meditate on John 4:1-26.

The Samaritan woman could not believe what she had just heard. Who was this man, this Jew who would speak to a woman from Samaria? And what he said!

For years, she had told people the half-truth that she had no husband. But now this total stranger had just said to her, "You are right when you say you have no husband. The fact is, you have had five husbands, and the man you now have is not your husband. What you have just said is quite true."

No one before had ever made her face the full truth of who she was. She tried changing the subject. Certainly she could get this Jew sidetracked into the perennial debate about where to worship. But no. Somehow he was managing to bring the subject back to truth: "God is spirit, and his worshipers must worship in spirit and in truth."

The woman said, "I know that Messiah is coming. When he comes, he will explain everything to us."

Then Jesus declared, "I who speak to you am he."

And Jesus wants to speak truth to us today. We all have facts about ourselves that we avoid facing. Some of us downplay our faults. Others of us devalue gifts God has given us. To the extent we deny who we are, we cannot worship God in truth. Are we willing to see ourselves as God sees us and let him bring us to wholeness?

———

19

Meditate on Mark 12:41-44.

The woman hurried to the Temple, hoping no one would notice her. She realized her clothes were worn, but they were the only things she owned. At least they were clean. Her rough, swollen fingers rubbed the two coins they held.

She reached the Temple and walked to the place where the offerings were put. Quickly, she dropped her coins into the offering and returned to her home. How God could use her measly offering she had no idea, but what little she had would always go to him.

The widow hadn't noticed the group of men across from the offering place. If she had, she wouldn't have intruded on their conversation. Two thousand years later, however, the words of one of the men are still being quoted: "I tell you the truth, this poor widow has put more into the treasury than all the others. They all gave out of their wealth; but she, out of her poverty, put in everything—all she had to live on."

It's too easy for us to judge the importance of our lives by human standards: The big offerings are the most important. Famous people can do the most for God. The more people who are involved, the more significant is the occasion.

The God who created our world does not *need* anything we can produce, but he will use it. To God, all of us are poor, but we are also worth the life of his Son. Like the widow, may we give God everything and trust him with the results.

20

Meditate on 1 John 2:15-17.

Loving the world is like trying to attract an elusive lover. The chase of the fantasy offers excitement. Did I look good enough? Did I act impressive yet detached? Will he choose me? We know what it will take to love and lure the world. If we set our sights on winning the affection of the world at any cost, we probably can.

Loving God is riskier, for it is more like loving my husband. The constancy of intimacy, rather than the chase of elusive love, brings lasting fulfillment. After years of marriage, my task is to continue to love my dear husband even when he doesn't do things just as I wish he would. We've lived in this house for more than two years, yet he still forgets what day the garbage must be hauled to the curb. He too knows my foibles, and he can tell when I'm bluffing or feel insecure. I can't hide behind a well-made-up face or crisply pressed clothes.

Loving God, like loving my husband, requires that I be painfully honest with myself and live my life one day at a time. Loving the world requires only that I look good and learn to count my riches. Sometimes I give in to my lust for the world until I see the face of the God whom I love, and I realize that after all these years we have a good thing going.

———

21

Meditate on 1 John 3:19-22.

This morning I reread my journal from a year that I remember most for its upheavals and setbacks. The entries surprised me. Many prayers for the people in my life and praises for God's presence are recorded in those pages. Time after time I acted out of love for my friends. Between the handwritten lines of daily happenings and hopes, there is a strength of faith that I didn't remember. Reading those pages that were written without censure infused my heart with confidence.

As one prone to believe that only excellent work counts, I tend to remember the times I failed more than the times I did my best to muddle faithfully through. How good God is to find ways to remind me that I am being molded and fashioned by love, when I can't see beyond my imperfections.

22

Meditate on 1 John 4:4-6.

First John says that "whoever knows God listens to us." My first response to this claim was rueful. Many times I've felt unheard and unheeded by other people of faith. But then I realized that listening has little to do with agreement. Listening means offering respectful attention to another's experience and beliefs. When we take time to listen to the spirit of another, we can sense whether God is present.

The writer of Psalm 42 uses the lyric phrase "deep calls to deep" to describe how two bodies of fathomless waters beckon to each other when God's power is made manifest. The metaphor reassures me that God's presence in my life brings with it an ability to discern when others truly share a deep desire for God.

This happened to me this year! When engulfed in loneliness and fear, I sought a spiritual companion who helped me listen to the churning depths of my despair. Only as I learned to listen to myself could I recognize who were the kindred spirits in my life. Deep speaks to deep when I take the time to listen.

———

23

Meditate on 1 John 4:13-16.

Love is God's address. It is where God lives. To abide in God means to dwell, inhabit, reside, and stay in love for God, for others, and for ourselves.

A woman told me a story today. She went to the bank and withdrew a large sum of money. Only when she went to purchase what she needed did she realize that she had been shortchanged. She said, "My first reaction was to doubt myself. I tried to convince myself that I must have lost the money somewhere, but in my heart I knew better. I had no way of proving that the bank didn't give me all my money. Yet I knew that if someone else had lost $100, I would come to their aid. Why was it so hard to love myself enough to right a wrong done to me?"

The woman mustered her confidence and returned to the bank. The teller asked if she would stay after the bank closed when the tills were counted. There was $100 extra in the tills!

In a simple way, that woman chose to live in the love God has for her by believing in herself.

———

24

Meditate on John 3:5.

The Gospel of John uses the metaphor of birth to describe the way we come into God's family, but makes it very clear that this is not like a human birth, dependent on sex and passion. Those who become children of God are "born, not of blood or of the will of the flesh or of the will of man, but of God" (John 1:13). These are the people who receive the true light, the Word who became flesh—Jesus Christ.

The part of the church I was brought up in emphasizes this image. We come into God's family by being "born again." But in reading the Gospels I have been fascinated to see that the only person who was told he needed to be born again was probably the most religiously moral person in Palestine. It was not the promiscuous woman at the well, not Zacchaeus the tax swindler, but Nicodemus—a Pharisee who kept the law, a member of the

Sanhedrin, and probably the foremost religious teacher.

As a young person reading my Bible, I always skipped over Jesus' condemnation of the Pharisees, because it didn't apply to me! I congratulated myself that I wasn't one of *them*, an enemy of Jesus! I was one of the good guys. I had accepted Christ as my Savior. I was keeping the rules.

But who was it who needed to be born again? Nicodemus did. I did. It's the "good" person, the religious person, the "superior" person, the person so caught in his or her standards that there is no way for the Spirit of God to penetrate that shell. It's the person who sees perfection as keeping all the right laws, doing the right things and not doing anything on the banned list.

Why did Nicodemus come to Jesus? According to John's chronology, he had seen and heard Jesus cleaning out the Temple. He had witnessed Jesus' passion for God and his fearless confrontation of set-in-its-ways authority that too often ignored God. To Nicodemus this must have seemed a breath from God. Jesus responded to his flattering greeting by answering his unspoken question: "Yes, if you want to see God at work, if you want to feel God's breath, you must open yourself to the wind of God's Spirit. Leave the old. Admit your poverty of spirit.

Let God do new things for you and change you from the inside out. Be willing to let go of all you thought you knew about God and come into God's family like a baby, who has to learn everything from scratch. Let God's Spirit fill you and teach you."

Lord, keep me from pride and mere moralism. I want to be open to the fresh wind of your Spirit.

———

25

Meditate on Matthew 6:21.

Some years ago when I took a new job in another city, I spent my first month living in rented quarters, so I could look for a house. The apartment was small and sparsely furnished. I had the barest amount of cookware and tableware, and nothing for entertainment. Living involved few choices. There was almost nothing to the housework, and nothing to tie me to the place. For those four weeks I had no investments in the place where I lived. I found it a most freeing experience.

But then I bought a house and moved my five rooms of furniture, plus kitchen, bath, and garage stuff. And I was caught again with a big house of earthly treasures—to which I have kept adding more.

Still, I keep hearing Jesus' words. Don't keep adding to your earthly treasures. Don't tie yourself to your possessions. They don't last. Your cloisonné will dent, your soapstone will shatter, your lovely china will break, your jewelry will be stolen. When I'm honest with myself, I know that my possessions possess me and my emotions, not so much out of fear that I'll lose them but rather tying me into a kind of cocoon that I keep winding around me. I'm not yet pure of heart in this realm of my life.

Our real home isn't here. Our real possessions are those we give away—the gifts we give in secret, the disciplines we practice quietly to connect us to our Father in heaven. And so I have to ask myself, "What have I given my heart to? Do I want to be free?"

Help me see you beyond my possessions, and so to possess them lightly as belonging ultimately to you.

———

Meditate on Matthew 7:24.

When it is time to buy a new house, what do you look for? Several women recently were discussing house-hunting. One wanted a large house to accommodate two offices. She and her husband are college professors and need their own spaces for research and writing. Another woman is a gourmet cook and dreams of having a house with an enormous kitchen. "A music room is a must for me and the children," said a third. Another quickly chimed in to say she wanted a two-story house with lots of insulation between the floors to dampen the noise of the loud rock music her children constantly play upstairs.

Some wanted other things—large trees, a nice yard with space for a vegetable or flower garden, compactness and easiness to care for. Price and location were mentioned more than once.

When my turn came, I said, "I like all the things

you've mentioned, but my house has to be a Thanksgiving house."

All of them wondered what I meant. What does a Thanksgiving house look like?

My husband and I have always liked driving through the country. Whenever we do, and I see a two-story farmhouse nestled in a clump of trees surrounded by beautiful meadows, I always say, "That's a Thanksgiving house!" Or sometimes we see a log cabin with smoke curling from the chimney, a stack of wood in the yard, and a dog or two on the porch, and I say, "That's a Thanksgiving house!"

Through the years of sighting such houses, I've learned that a true Thanksgiving house can be of almost any style. It can be large or small, Colonial or modern, brick or board.

Perhaps I can explain it better. A Thanksgiving house is the kind that puts a glow over the people we love. It's a place where sorrows are quickly turned into joys; one that lets us be childlike and allows laughter to permeate its structure; one where holidays and holy days are shared, where memories are made and traditions grow. It's a haven of love, warmth, and security.

A Thanksgiving house can be any type of house, but there is one rule that is set in concrete: It has to be a house built on a solid relationship with God; a place where God's promises and presence are duly noted; a house where celebration seems natural because God is there.

Bless this house, O Lord, we pray;
Make it a Thanksgiving house by night and day.

27

Meditate on Romans 8:27.

A few years ago, our family moved to another city and had the good fortune of looking at houses with a wonderful real estate agent. In a week's time, we must have gone through at least seventy-five houses.

At every house, the agent rang the doorbell. If the occupants were not at home, she worked the combination on the lockbox attached to the house, removed a key, and proceeded to open a lock on the front or side door.

After we entered the house, we encountered more locks. There were sliding locks on windows, safety locks on patio doors, deadbolt locks on basement doors. Sometimes there were locks on garages or outbuildings.

In some homes, we were shown sophisticated security systems that ensured safety against intruders who might attempt to break through one of the many locks.

Locks are, unfortunately, a necessity in our homes, cars, stores, and churches. I know of one church that not only has locks and bolts on all its doors, but also has five security guards who patrol the parking lots and building at all hours of the day and night.

Anywhere there is a threat to safety, we need the protection and security of a system of locks and safeguards.

But there are some locks in life that are a disadvantage. These are the locks on our personal lives that are so tightly fastened that growth, caring, and sharing are inhibited and stifled, if not totally eliminated.

Think how people become when icy locks around their hearts keep out love. Or maybe you know some folks who maintain a grudge lock that keeps out forgiveness. There are some people who hold tightly to a stingy lock that forbids the entrance of compassion and generosity. And many people lock up the rooms of their lives with a restrictive lock to keep out the presence of God. Sometimes locks cause us to lose our real sense of perspective on life.

Father, you have the key to open the locks of my heart, mind, and being. Give me the wisdom, humility, and courage to place my complete trust in the Master Locksmith and to leave my house wide open to you at all times.

———

28

Meditate on Luke 12:27.

I have spent months trying to locate an affordable spinning wheel. Last fall some friends and I were going through an antique store in California where there was a little room filled with assorted spinning wheels. Some were very old, and others were new. Some were large, and others were small.

The owner was carding some wool in preparation for spinning it into yarn. When she finished the combing process, she spun the strands on an old-fashioned wheel that would take only one thread at a time. Fortunately, this wasn't her only method of getting material, as it was for women in colonial days.

When I showed an interest in the wheels, she asked if I knew how to spin. I admitted that my sole interest in owning a spinning wheel was to have it as a decoration in my den. But my inability at spinning wool didn't lessen the fascination I felt at watching her expertly turning raw wool into usable yarn.

As I watched, I let my imagination take over. I imagined that God was sitting at a giant spinning wheel and that we were the raw material out of which he was to make something. I imagined God carefully combing out our matted, unusable traits of selfishness, jealousy, and malice; and doing it with gentleness and patience.

I could see God bringing order as, one at a time, he spun out and untangled our knotted threads of pride and self-importance. I visualized God delicately coloring each thread so that we would coordinate with the overall design he had planned for us and our world.

I thought what a big difference it would make if only we allowed God to be the Master Spinner in every aspect of our lives. He has done so beautifully with so many things.

Jesus said, "Consider the lilies of the field . . . ; "they toil not, neither do they spin: and yet . . . Solomon in all his glory was not arrayed like one of these" (Matthew 6:28-29 KJV).

If we let the heavenly Spinner take over for us, we will become material for his beautifully hand-crafted products. Who knows? Our lives may even be more beautiful than the lilies!

29

Meditate on Joshua 1:5.

In the fall of the year, when I was expecting our first child, we turned the spare bedroom of our small house into a nursery. It was so much fun planning it and, bit by bit, getting it ready for our new baby.

We bought a Boston rocker. My father-in-law found an antique cherry cradle and refinished it for us. I made a baby-sized, pastel patchwork quilt. My mother-in-law brought us a bathinette with built-in storage space under it. My mother and I sewed an extensive layette. We hung pictures and mobiles suitable for a baby's environment.

The finished room looked like a little bit of heaven, and the arrival of the baby only reinforced that impression. What a joy it was for us to rock, clothe, feed, and comfort our wonderful son in a room that was lovingly prepared and decorated just for him.

Sometimes I need God to have a nursery room

specially outfitted and decorated just for me. I know I'm an adult, but when I cry over hurt feelings I want to craw into God's lap and be rocked. When my soul is dry and hungry, I long for God to feed me soothing words. When daily cares have exhausted me and made me anxious, I need God to sing me to sleep. When I feel unsure of myself, I yearn for God's strong arms to steady me and hold me up.

When I am feeling alone and unlovely, I desperately need to hear God say, "I will never fail you nor forsake you." When I feel afraid, I want to cry out, "Come into my life where I am hurting, Lord. Please hold my hand. You know the joy your comfort can bring. You understand."

It is amazing how all the burdens and cares of life can disappear when I become God's little child.

———

30

Meditate on 1 Corinthians 14:33.

Some people collect jewelry boxes. They don't necessarily put anything in them; they simply enjoy the unique characteristics of the various boxes they have.

Jewelry boxes are fascinating. Some have small sealed divisions that hide secret compartments. Boxes with musical mechanisms give a special kind of pleasure each time they are opened. And some boxes are beautifully handcrafted, with wooden inlays, dovetailed joints, or carved figures.

My jewelry box isn't anything particularly unusual, but it holds many fond memories. It is filled with trinkets I have acquired through the years. A few are valuable, I suppose, but most are simply enjoyable ornaments given to me by family members and friends.

When our youngest son was a small child, it delighted him to have the task of straightening

Mommy's jumbled-up jewelry box. He would get into the center of the bed with the box and begin his work. After carefully untangling the chains and beads, he would lay each item out with special care. Then he would bestow on the assembled lot the kind of admiration usually reserved for the crown jewels themselves.

Then the questions would begin: "Mommy, where did you get this necklace? Who gave you this bracelet? When did you get these earrings?"

Every time, he asked the same questions, persisting in the litany until the very last trinket was replaced in the box. But when he had completed his task, order was restored to my jewelry box for a while, and we had a wonderful time of sharing.

Sometimes, I confess, I feel as if my life is like a jumbled-up jewelry box. I keep anger stored up in little secret compartments. I grope through a maze of partitions in search of parts of myself I can't find. I get tangled up in frustrations. I feel trapped because the key to my existence seems to be lost.

That's when I need God to step in and straighten out everything. I need to hear: "Child, vent your pent-up anger by praying for the people in situations that have hurt you. You'll be amazed at how quickly your anger will vanish.

"Little ones, when you feel that you are at a dead

end, follow my road. Its sign clearly reads, 'I am the way, the truth, and the life. Follow me.'

"Try to replace your frustrations with a little more self-esteem. Remember, you are worth more to me than precious stones.

"You may have thought you lost the key to your life, but the Creator always holds the master key. Keep your faith in me."

It is amazing what God can do for our complicated situations if only we let him.

Thank you, Lord, for the order you restore to my life.

———

31

Meditate on Daniel 2:20-22.

The patio had a somber look yesterday. The furniture was covered in plastic for the winter. The barbecue grill was packed away in the basement. A few late-blooming chrysanthemums drooped on their tired, drying stalks. It was a lonesome sight.

The sky had a dismal look, too. The normally blue background with fluffy white clouds gave way to a dull pewter color with dark, heavy clouds hovering so close to the ground that you felt as if you would freeze if you touched them.

My spirit had a dejected feeling. There was a sense of constriction around my head, as if I were wearing a cap of depression. My energy level dropped to what must have been an all-time low. The sounds of music in my heart fell silent. I was grateful for the arrival of evening and the chance to go to sleep and shut out the melancholy day.

Today the patio looks different. The snow that fell

stealthily during the night left a coat of white icing on the plastic furniture covers. The old chrysanthemums now appear to glow as beautiful bronze blossoms under a generous sprinkling of powdered sugar. The entire patio looks radiant.

The sky looks different today too. The sun, shining golden white against a field of azure blue, bestows its gentle warmth over the whole enchanted world.

Best of all, my spirit has a different feeling today. Winter arrived so softly and quietly on our late autumn patio last night. How beautiful it is this morning! God has sent a miracle from heaven that makes my heart lift with love and cheer. My spirit is sparkling!

> *Blessed be the name of God for ever, . . .*
> *He changes the times and seasons . . .*
> *he reveals deep and mysterious things; . . .*
> *and the light dwells with him.* (RSV)